D0315184

MY FIRST ENCYCLOPEDIA

An eye-catching series of information books designed to encourage young children to find out more about the world around them. Each one is carefully prepared by a subject specialist with the help of experienced writers and educational advisers.

KINGFISHER
Kingfisher Publications Plc
New Penderel House, 283-288 High Holborn, London WC1V 7HZ

First published in paperback by Kingfisher Publications Plc 1994
2 4 6 8 10 9 7 5 3
2TR/1BP/0600/SF/(FR)/135MA

Originally published in hardback under the series title Young World
This edition © copyright Kingfisher Publications Plc 2000
Text & Illustrations © copyright Kingfisher Publications Plc 1992

ISBN 1 85697 259 3

Phototypeset by Waveney Typesetters, Norwich
Printed in China

MY FIRST ENCYCLOPEDIA

Dinosaurs

Kingfisher

Author
Michael Benton

Educational consultant
Daphne Ingram

Series consultant
Brian Williams

Editor
Camilla Hallinan

Designer
Brian Robertson

Illustrators
Marion Appleton (pages 112-113)
Bob Bampton (pages 108-109)
Richard Draper (pages 28-29, 32-33, 64-65)
Tim Hayward (pages 26-27, 66-67, 74-77, 98-103)
Tony Kenyon (pages 80-81, 100-101)
Terence Lambert (pages 84-95)
Bernard Long (pages 68-73, 78-79, 82-83)
Shirley Mallinson (pages 12-13, 16-18, 26-27, 34-38,
45, 47-48, 50, 56-57, 80-81, 90, 114-119)
Robert Morton (pages 24-25, 104-107)
Ann Winterbotham (pages 14-15, 20-23, 28-29, 32-61)

About this book

Everyone has heard of dinosaurs, and everyone knows that they lived a long time ago. But is it true that they all were big and stupid? Every year people find new clues to what the dinosaurs were *really* like...

One surprise is that dinosaurs lived all over the world, even near the North and South Poles. Another surprise is that some dinosaurs were as small as a chicken, as fast as a racehorse and clever too.

One of the best things about dinosaurs is that there is still a lot to find out about them and about the animals that lived before and after them. What colour were the dinosaurs? Why did they disappear? Were they killed by a giant meteorite when it crashed into Earth? Read this book to discover amazing facts and puzzling questions about animals long ago.

CONTENTS

LONG AGO

ALL KINDS OF DINOSAURS

DINOSAUR DAYS

EVOLUTION

Long ago

🦕 Meeting dinosaurs

You can see all kinds of dinosaurs in a museum. But no one has ever seen one alive. Museum dinosaurs are models and skeletons.

The real dinosaurs lived millions of years ago. Then they became extinct. That means they died out, for ever.

Deinonychus model

model of
Tyrannosaur
rex's head

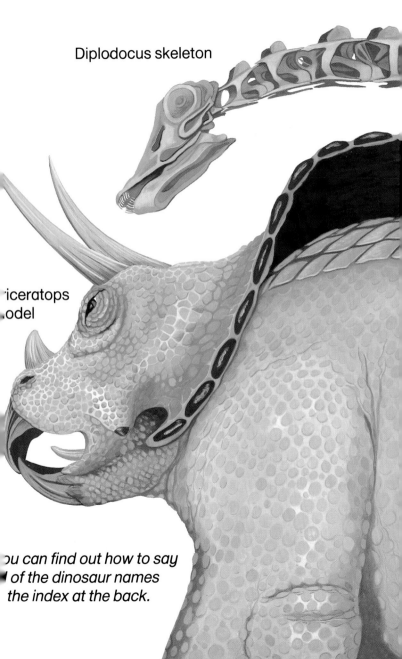

Diplodocus skeleton

...iceratops
...odel

...ou can find out how to say
...l of the dinosaur names
...the index at the back.

🦕 Dinosaur world

Allosaurus

Stegosaurus

Dryosaurus

This scene shows some dinosaurs in North America 150 million years ago. Stegosaurus might have made a good mea for Allosaurus. But big Brachiosaurus wa quite safe.

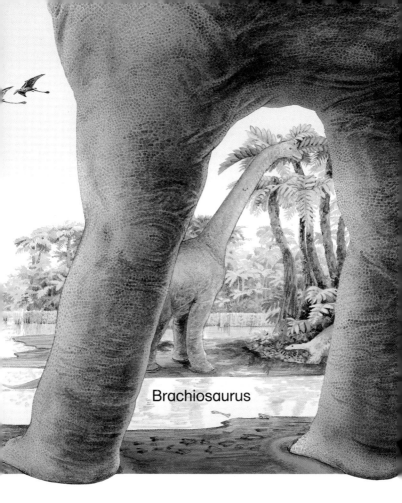
Brachiosaurus

t the time of the dinosaurs there were no
eople, no cameras to take photographs,
o wildlife films. But we know about
inosaurs because of clues they left behind.

🦕 Dinosaur clues

We know about dinosaurs mainly from their bones. But there are other clues. They all help scientists to work out what dinosaurs looked like and how they lived.

Sometimes prints of dinosaur skin are found. The prints were made in soft mud millions of years ago. The mud has hardened into rock.

Iguanodon model,
1853

New discoveries change our ideas about what dinosaurs looked like.

Teeth and claws tell us what dinosaurs ate. Footprints show the shape of the foot, and even how fast the dinosaur ran.

Some of the rarest finds are dinosaur eggs and nests. Sometimes a baby's skeleton is still inside.

1853, people thought
uanodon had a horn
its nose. Now we
now the horn was a
ike on its thumb.

now

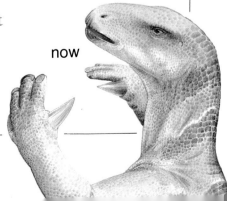

🦕 Studying dinosaurs

Dinosaur bones lie buried in rock.
Scientists called palaeontologists dig up th
bones and study them.

Palaeontologists try to fit the bones
together, and work out what the dinosaur
looked like. They can tell the age of the
bones from the age of the rock they were
buried in.

All kinds of

dinosaurs

One of the first dinosaurs was Coelophysi
It was about as tall as a ten-year-old child
It lived about 220 million years ago, in
North America. Scientists call this time th
Triassic Period.

Coelophysis was a reptile. Reptiles have scaly skin, and they lay eggs. Lizards, snakes and crocodiles are some of the reptiles that live today.

The word dinosaur means 'terrible lizard'. Like the lizards, all dinosaurs were reptiles.

🦕 Big and small

Some dinosaurs were huge. Seismosaurus was the biggest. If it were alive today, and you stood at the end of its tail, you could hardly see to the top of its head. Its name means 'earth-shaker', and it probably weighed up to 90 tonnes!

Diplodocus

Diplodocus was one of the longest dinosaurs – 30 metres long! That about the same length as three buses bumper to bumper.

Compsognathus

Seismosaurus

Brachiosaurus

Big Brachiosaurus
ate only plants.
So did Diplodocus
and Seismosaurus.

Tyrannosaurus rex

Tyrannosaurus rex ate other animals.
This monster was the biggest meat-eater
ver. Compsognathus was a meat-eater
oo. But it was only the size of a turkey.

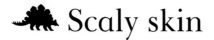 # Scaly skin

Scientists know the size of dinosaurs because they find their bones.
No one has ever found dinosaur skin.
Sometimes, though, rocks show prints made by the skin.

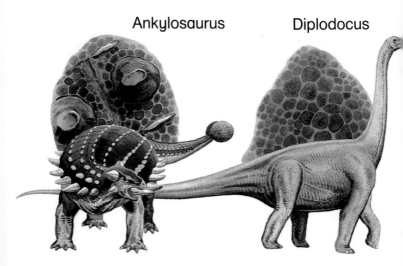

Ankylosaurus Diplodocus

Some dinosaurs had big knobbly plates and some had small smooth scales.

Skin prints do not show what colour the dinosaurs were. Perhaps dinosaurs had the same colours as modern reptiles.

Coral snakes have bright stripes to warn off meat-eaters: their poison can kill. But desert snakes are a dull colour: they can hide in the sand.

coral snake

desert snake

Collared lizards have different markings to show which is the male and which is the female.

female

male

baby

Alligators change colour as they grow.

adult

Lizard hips, bird hips

Scientists sort all the dinosaurs into two groups, saurischians and ornithischians. Hip bones show which group a dinosaur belongs to.

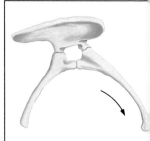

saurischian hip

In saurischians, the front hip bone points forwards. In ornithischians it points back.

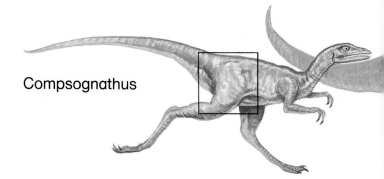

Compsognathus

Saurischian means 'lizard hip'.
This group includes some plant-eaters and all the meat-eaters. Compsognathus was a saurischian.

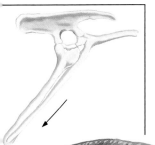

ornithischian hip

Ornithischian means 'bird hip'. Ornithischians were all plant-eaters. Protoceratops was an ornithischian.

Protoceratops

'alaeontologists think that there were
bout 500 species or types of dinosaurs –
00 saurischian species and 300
rnithischian species.

Sorting dinosaurs

There are many kinds of dinosaurs. So the two main groups are divided into smaller groups.

The saurischian group splits into meat-eating theropods and plant-eating sauropodomorphs.

sauropods

prosauropods

theropods

sauropodomorphs

SAURISCHIANS

meat-eaters

plant-eaters

The ornithischian group splits into five:
ankylosaurs, stegosaurs, ornithopods,
ceratopsians and pachycephalosaurs.
These were all plant-eaters.

rnithopods

ceratopsians

pachycephalosaurs

stegosaurs

ankylosaurs

ORNITHISCHIANS

RS

Amazing facts

Richard Owen invented the word dinosaur in 1842. At the time, he knew of just three species.

Every year, about ten new species of dinosaurs are named. They come from al over the world.

The oldest dinosaur we know was named Eoraptor in 1993. It lived about 22 million years ago. It was only one metre long, but it was a fierce meat-eater.

Eoraptor's name means 'dawn-stealer because it was born at the beginning or dawn of the dinosaur age and it grabbed small animals to eat.

Some scientists wonder if the biggest dinosaurs needed more than one heart to pump blood around their massive bodies.

Dinosaur

days

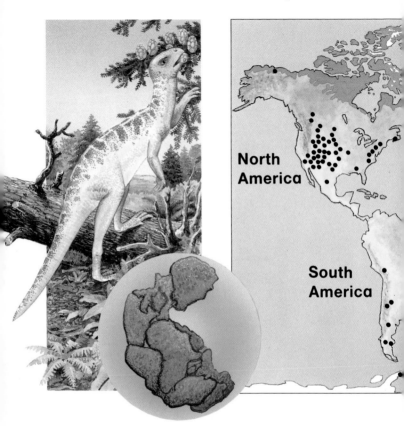

Hypsilophodon's bones are found as far apart as Antarctica, Australia and England. When the dinosaurs were alive the continents were joined together in a single land called Pangaea.

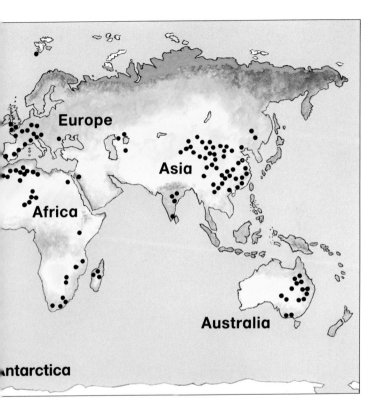

Dinosaurs lived all over Pangaea. We
know this because their bones are found on
every continent. The dots on the map show
where they have been dug up. Can you
find a site close to where you live?

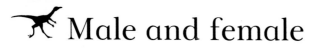 # Male and female

Skulls show that the
male Parasaurolophus
had a longer crest than
the female. Male
dinosaurs may have
used their crests and
horns for showing off
to the females.

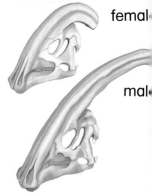

female

male

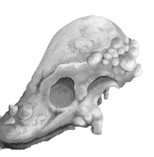

Pachycephalosaurus had a very thick skull top. The males probably crashed heads in fights to win a female.
Wild sheep fight in the same way now.

Nests and eggs

Dinosaurs laid eggs, as modern reptiles do. We know how they did this because of fantastic nests found in North America.

Maiasaura scraped the ground
to make a big nest.
She laid up to 30 eggs
in the nest, in neat circles.

dinosaur nest

Then Maiasaura covered her eggs with leaves and ferns, and some soil. This made a kind of compost heap to keep the eggs warm. Now Maiasaura had to protect her eggs from hungry meat-eaters.

Other Maiasaura built their nests nearby. They all helped to keep watch, to stop Oviraptor stealing eggs.

Dinosaur babies

Some very rare finds
show what a dinosaur
baby looked like inside
its egg.

unhatched
baby

Maiasaura babies probably all hatched at
about the same time. They already had
tiny teeth for chewing. Their parents
brought them tasty little bits of food.

Maiasaura babies were small and weak at first. So they stayed in the nest until they were big enough to look after themselves.

But others were ready to leave their nest and search for food right away. How do we know? From looking at the egg shells.

Maiasaura egg shells were trampled into tiny pieces by all the babies in the nest. But Hypsilophodon babies quickly left their nest. So their shells were not as badly damaged.

In a herd

Many dinosaurs grew up and lived in large groups called herds. The dinosaurs in the herd protected one another.

A fierce Tyrannosaurus is attacking this herd of Triceratops. What can they do? The babies and the weaker animals huddle together in the middle.

The big males stand in a
circle around the herd,
and point their sharp
horns outwards. They
look ready to fight.

Tyrannosaurus gives up. But it will be
back, on the look-out for a stray baby or a
sick or old animal that can't keep up with
the herd.

41

Noisy dinosaurs

Dinosaurs made all kinds of loud noises. The hadrosaurs, the duck-billed dinosaurs were very noisy. They honked and hooted and tooted through their noses.

Edmontosaurus had some extra-stretchy skin on top of its broad nose. This could fill with air and vibrate to make sounds. A frog croaks with a stretchy pouch in its throat. But Edmontosaurus was much bigger and much louder than any frog.

Parasaurolophus was another duck-billed dinosaur. It had hollow breathing tubes inside its amazing crest. So when it breathed out hard, Parasaurolophus tooted like a trumpet or a trombone.

Scientists have made models of the skulls to test the sounds they make, and they work!

All kinds of animals call out to find one another, or to give warnings to one another. Dinosaurs must have done the same.

Looking for food

Many plant-eating dinosaurs travelled long distances in herds of up to a hundred animals. They were looking for new grazing places. How do we know? The evidence comes from rock covered with many footprints.

The footprints show that dozens of
Apatosaurus walked by, all heading
the same way, millions of years
ago. The young animals
walked in the middle,
safe from attack.

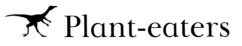 Plant-eaters

Most dinosaurs were herbivores, which means they ate plants. There was no grass then, but there were many kinds of leaves, fruits, roots and cones to feed on.

Edmontosaurus and the other duck-bills were plant-eaters.

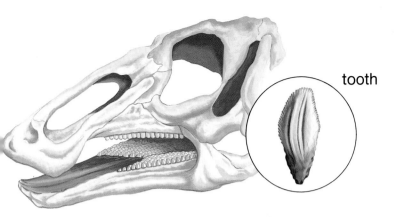

tooth

dmontosaurus' skull had a wide bony
eak at the front, for nipping bits off a
lant. Dozens, even hundreds, of teeth
ned the jaws near the back. These were
sed for chewing and grinding the food.

dmontosaurus' teeth were worn down by
l the chewing and grinding. So new teeth
ere always growing.

ome plant-eaters swallowed
ebbles, just as birds swallow
rit, to help grind up the
ood in their stomachs.
cientists call them
omach stones.

47

 Meat-eaters

Some dinosaurs were carnivores, which means they ate meat. Small meat-eaters fed on lizards, frogs, and other small animals. Others were big enough to feed on other dinosaurs.

Meat-eaters had strong jaws. Their teeth were pointed and curved backwards, good for tearing flesh. The edges had sharp zig zags, like the blade of a steak knife.

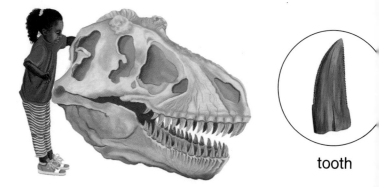

tooth

The biggest meat-eater was Tyrannosaurus rex. It could have swallowed you in a couple of mouthfuls!

Going hunting

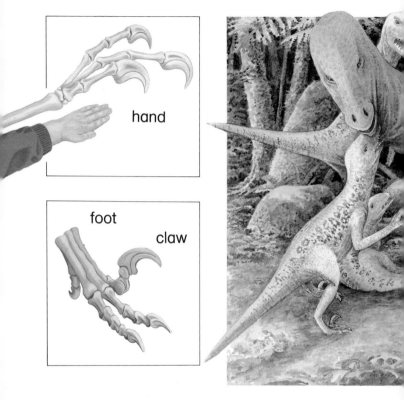

hand

foot

claw

Deinonychus was a ferocious meat-eater.
It had long fingers to grip its prey, the
animal it attacked. And it had a terrible
slashing claw on its back feet. The claw
tore the animal's flesh.

Deinonychus was less than two metres tall, about the size of a human adult. So it hunted in a pack to catch larger dinosaurs. The pack would corner the prey, bring it to the ground, and kill it.

🦖 Dinosaur defences

Plant-eaters had to defend themselves from the meat-eaters.

Triceratops had three horns for fighting off a meat-eater. And a large bony shield protected its neck from attack.

Triceratops

Iguanodon had two sharp thumb spikes. A nasty stab from one of those would scare off the enemy!

Iguanodon

Even the giants such as Diplodocus needed defences. Diplodocus could lash its long tail like a whip to keep the meat-eaters away.

Ankylosaurus had a shorter tail. But a whack from the bony club on the end would hurt a lot.

Diplodocus

Ankylosaurus also had bony armour over its back and head. So this big plant-eater was safe from most meat-eaters.

Ankylosaurus

53

Clever or stupid?

People used to think that dinosaurs were not very clever. This was because dinosaur skulls have only a small space for a brain.

Stegosaurus weighed six or seven tonnes, so it was as heavy as an elephant. But it had a brain the size of a walnut.

Perhaps Stegosaurus did not need a big brain. After all, it was big and safe from most attackers, and it spent most of the day grazing slowly.

brain

Other dinosaurs had bigger brains.

Stenonychosaurus was a fast little meat-eater. It had big eyes and a good sense of smell for finding small animals to eat. It had long, strong fingers for grabbing them too. Because Stenonychosaurus was a hunter, it needed a bigger brain.

✗ On the move

Running away, or chasing the next meal, some dinosaurs were fast. Struthiomimus could run as fast as a racehorse.

Footprints in rock show how dinosaurs walked and ran.

Iguanodon went down on all fours when it was walking. But it rose up on its back legs when it was running.

Scientists work out a dinosaur's speed by looking at the length of its legs and at its tracks. The faster the dinosaur ran, the bigger the spaces between its footprints.

The big meat-eater Megalosaurus left huge three-toed footprints. They show that it always went around on its back legs.

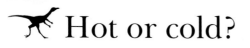

Hot or cold?

Stegosaurus

Reptiles are cold-blooded. Dinosaurs were reptiles, so were they cold-blooded? Scientists are not sure.

Cold-blooded animals do not make heat inside their bodies. If the air around them is warm, they are warm and active. If the air is cold, the are cold and sluggish. Warm-blooded animals stay warm and active even if the air is cold, because their bodies *do* make heat.

Perhaps Stegosaurus was cold-blooded. Perhaps the plates on its back soaked up the sun's heat in the morning, and lost heat if it got too warm later on.

But maybe big, slow dinosaurs were too big to change temperature and were warm-blooded.

Diplodocus

Maybe small, active
dinosaurs were
warm-blooded too.

Deinonychus

59

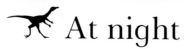

When the sun went down and the
temperature dropped, dinosaurs probably
found somewhere to lie down and sleep.

Then it was safe for warm-blooded
mammals to come out of their burrows and
hunt for insects and tasty fruit.

1

2

3

4

n the morning, when the sun came up,
Tyrannosaurus would have grunted and
stretched as the warmth crept into its
body. This huge animal must have used its
tiny arms for balance as it got up. First it
straightened its back legs. Then it pushed
its head back and swung itself upright.

Amazing facts

The last part of the world to reveal dinosaur bones was Antarctica. An ankylosaur was found in the ice in 1987. But it hasn't been named yet.

Nests of eggs were first found in the Mongolian desert, in China. The eggs belonged to Protoceratops. An American expedition found them in the 1920s.

Scientists used to think duck-billed dinosaurs spent most of the time in water, like ducks. They thought Parasaurolophus used its long crest like a snorkel, to breathe when it was under water. But no one agrees with these ideas any more.

Dinosaur footprints were first found around 1800 in North America. People thought they were made by giant birds. But now we know they belonged to a dinosaur called Anchisaurus.

Evolution

How long ago?

Dinosaurs were not the first animals that ever lived.

Imagine the age of the Earth as one day and night on a clock. It's midnight now.

Humans appeared at about one minute to midnight. So we have only just arrived! Dinosaurs appeared just before eleven. But there were other animals long before the dinosaurs.

The Earth is
very, very old.
It formed 4,600
million years ago.

Life began in the oceans.
Tiny cells called algae and
bacteria were the first living
things. They were the first
plants and animals.

Bigger plants and animals
developed from these cells.
This process is called evolution.
On land, dinosaurs evolved 230
million years ago, and died out
65 million years ago.

The first humans
lived five
million
years ago.

✕ The first animals

The first traces of life appeared in the sea
3,500 million years ago. That was a long
time before dinosaurs roamed the land.

algae

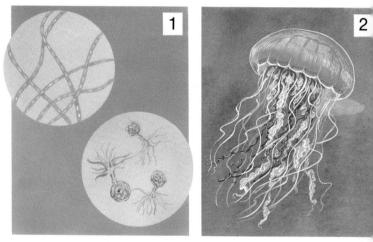

bacteria   jellyfish

Tiny single cells were the earliest plants
and animals. They were similar to modern
algae and bacteria. Later came much
larger animals, such as jellyfish. Then
animals with shells evolved.

The trilobite is extinct now. That means there is none alive today. But other species evolved which looked like animals living in the sea today.

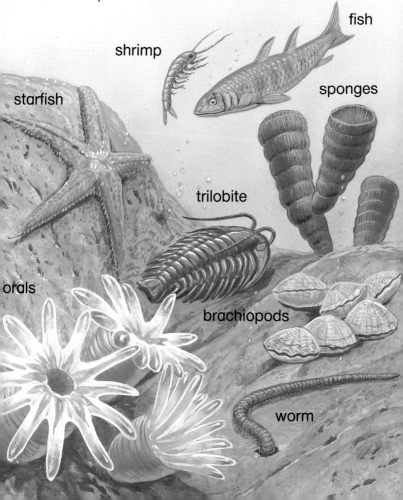

fish

shrimp

sponges

starfish

trilobite

corals

brachiopods

worm

Under water

Fish were the first animals with bones. All the other bony animals, including dinosaurs and ourselves, have evolved from fish.

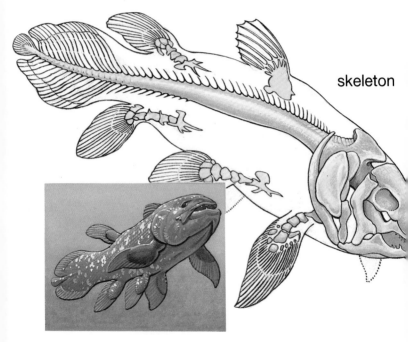

skeleton

The first coelacanths lived 400 million years ago. There are still coelacanths today, in seas off Africa.

The earliest fish were covered in bony
armour. Dunkleosteus was a giant meat-
eating fish, the terror of the seas.

⌁ Onto the land

About 380 million years ago, some fish moved onto land. Fins for swimming evolved into legs with toes for walking. Ichthyostega had seven toes on its back legs. These new animals were amphibians.

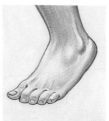

The amphibians could live on land and in fresh water, but not in the salty sea. Some amphibians ate spiders and insects that already lived on the land. Eogyrinus fed on fish in the lakes.

Diplocaulus had a very odd head. Perhaps the two wide 'horns' helped it swim more quickly, or stopped other animals swallowing it.

❧ The first reptiles

After the amphibians
came the reptiles.

Amphibians lay their
eggs in water. The eggs
are soft like jelly, and
hatch into tiny
tadpoles.

Reptiles lay their eggs
on dry land. Inside the
hard eggshell, the baby
feeds on the yolk until it
is big enough to hatch.

Hylonomus was one of the
first reptiles. It lived 320
million years ago in Canada.
It was 20 centimetres long.

Dimetrodon was
much bigger,
three metres
long.
You can see why
scientists call it
a sailback.

Perhaps the sail caught the sunshine in the
morning, to help Dimetrodon warm up. If
Dimetrodon got too hot in the midday sun,
perhaps the sail could then release heat.

Back to the sea

Some reptiles went back into the sea to find their food. These sea reptiles lived during the age of the dinosaurs. The nothosaurs could live on land and in the sea. They may have had webbed feet, to push through the water like paddles.

The ichthyosaurs looked like large dolphins. They had flippers instead of legs, and the tail had a tall upright fin.

Ichthyosaurs could not go onto land to lay eggs. So they gave birth to their babies under water. A skeleton has been found that has a baby coming out tail first.

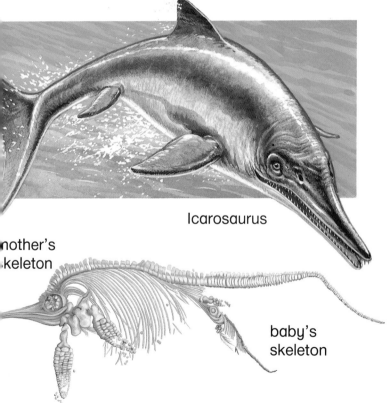

Icarosaurus

mother's skeleton

baby's skeleton

Ocean food

The oceans were full of food for the sea reptiles. This placodont fed on oysters and other hard-shelled animals. First it snipped shells off the rocks with its long front teeth. Then it crushed the shells with massive, flat, back teeth.

It spat out the shells before it swallowed the flesh.

Many sea reptiles ate ammonites. Ammonites are creatures with coiled shells of all shapes and sizes. Sometimes their shells are found with tooth marks!

 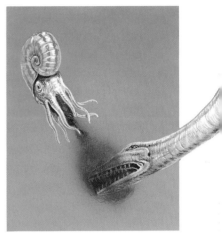

An ammonite was like an octopus. It gathered food with long arms called tentacles. It had large eyes, and when it saw danger it darted away by squirting a jet of water. It could even squirt a cloud of dark ink to distract its enemy while it escaped.

 A long neck

Some of the sea reptiles had the best of both worlds. Tanystropheus could hunt food on land, and catch fish from the sea.

Tanystropheus had an amazing neck that could reach deep into the water. There were only 12 bones in its neck. But each bone was up to 30 centimetres long. (The bones in your neck are only two centimetres long.)

The babies had shorter necks.
They fed on insects.
As they grew, their necks
became longer and longer.
Then they could start
catching fish.

Heads or tails?

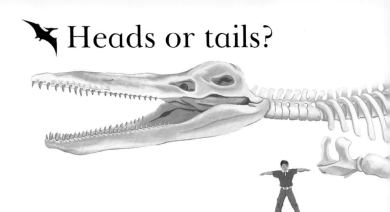

Plesiosaurs and pliosaurs were sea reptiles that lived during the age of dinosaurs. Pliosaurs had huge heads, short necks and long tails. Plesiosaurs had smaller heads, long necks and short tails.

An American palaeontologist, Edward Cope, once made a model of Elasmosaurus. But he got it wrong.

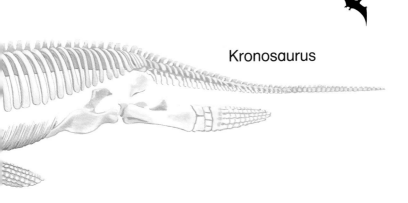

Kronosaurus

Kronosaurus was a pliosaur, and it was one of the biggest. It was 15 metres long, and its massive skull is about the size of a big car.

In 1870 his rival, Othniel Marsh, showed that Cope had put the plesiosaur's head on the end of its tail.

Turtles and crocodiles

Many of the ancient land and sea reptiles died out long ago. But lizards, snakes, turtles and crocodiles are still here.

Archelon was a monster turtle, four metres long. It swam in the seas that covered part of North America 100 million years ago. Its big paddles made it a fast swimmer.

Deinosuchus was another monster, bigger than any crocodile alive today. The biggest measured 16 metres from nose to tail.

The first crocodiles lived over 215 million years ago, about the same time as the dinosaurs. No wonder these terrible reptiles ruled land and sea.

Flying reptiles

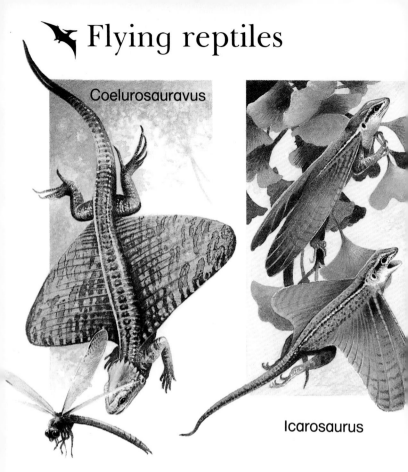

Coelurosauravus

Icarosaurus

Some reptiles took to the air, 250 million years ago. At first they were gliders. Their wings kept them up in the air as they leapt from tree to tree, but they did not flap and they had no feathers.

Longisquama

The first gliders' wings grew out from their
sides and were held up on long ribs. But
Longisquama had tall crests along its
back. The crests might have opened out
like wings and helped it to glide.

85

Wings without feathers

The first true flying reptiles
were the pterosaurs. Each
wing was a thin sheet of
skin stretched along the
arm and one very
long finger.

Pterosaurs were
warm-blooded, and
their bodies and
wings were covered
with short fur,
like bats.

Dimorphodon

Most pterosaurs were fish-eaters.
They scooped fish out of the sea, and swallowed them whole.

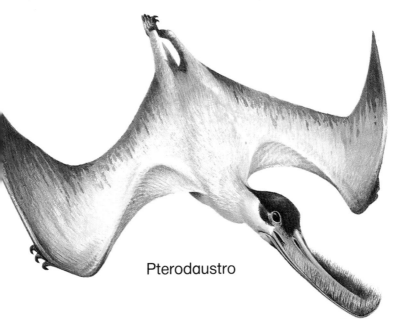

Rhamphorhynchus

Pterodaustro from Argentina had thousands of thin, bendy teeth that sieved small animals out of the water.

Pterodaustro

Giants of the air

Pteranodon

The largest pterosaurs were more like aeroplanes than birds in size!

Pteranodon was from North America. It soared high above a great sea that ran from Mexico to Alaska. This giant had wings that measured seven metres from tip to tip.

Quetzalcoatlus

The biggest flying animal of all
time was Quetzalcoatlus.

A Quetzalcoatlus skeleton was found in
Texas, in the 1970s. This pterosaur had a
human-sized body, and the widest wings
ever seen: about 12 metres from tip to tip.

89

Is it a bird?

In 1860, workers found the impression of a feather in a quarry in Germany. Even one feather meant there must have been a bird there. But what did that bird look like?

One year later, a whole skeleton was found. The rock showed that it once had feathers on the wings and along the tail. It was 150 million years old. So it lived at the same time as the dinosaurs. This first bird was called Archaeopteryx. Its name means 'ancient wing'.

Many scientists think that dinosaurs were the ancestors of modern birds. Look at Eoraptor, for example. It is the oldest dinosaur we know. It has a similar shape to Archaeopteryx and to a modern bird such as a roadrunner.

Eoraptor

Archaeopteryx

roadrunner

Learning to fly

How did flying reptiles and birds learn to fly? Perhaps they learned to flap their wings as they leapt from tree to tree.

When they chased insects for food,
perhaps they flapped their wings to soar
off the ground and high into the air.

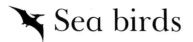 Sea birds

Modern birds have
no teeth. But the
first birds had teeth
that were small and
sharp.

Ichthyornis lived 70 million years after
Archaeopteryx. It was a sea bird. So it
may have lived like a gull, soaring over the
waves and diving for fish.

1

2

Hesperornis was another sea bird. It lived at the same time as Ichthyornis. But it had no proper wings and it could not fly.

Hesperornis probably lived like a penguin. Instead of flying, it slid off a rock, swam out to sea and dived deep down in search of fish.

Ichthyornis and Hesperornis both had short, strong legs with webbed feet. This made them powerful swimmers.

1

2

Amazing facts

Ichthyosaurs had rings of bone around their big eyeballs. This helped to protect the eyes from pressure when the animals dived deep for fish.

The first turtles had teeth. Turtles today have no teeth, only a sharp beak.

Crocodile ancestors ran on their back legs and fed on insects. It was only later that they became fish-eating swimmers.

Archaeopteryx may not be the oldest bird. An animal called Protoavis has been found in Texas, in North America. It lived 50 million years before Archaeopteryx. But not everyone agrees that it is a bird.

The first Archaeopteryx skeleton was sold to the British Museum in 1864 for £700. It is worth millions today.

After the

dinosaurs

Dinosaurs disappear

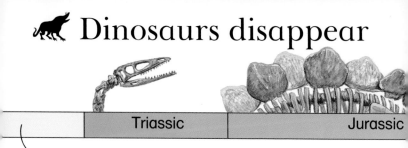

	Triassic	Jurassic

PALAEOZOIC

MESOZOI◄

Dinosaurs roamed the world for 165 million years, from the Triassic Period to the end of the Cretaceous Period. This time is called the Mesozoic Era. No dinosaur bones are found from after the Mesozoic Era. That is because the dinosaurs became extinct. So did the great sea reptiles, the ammonites and the pterosaurs.

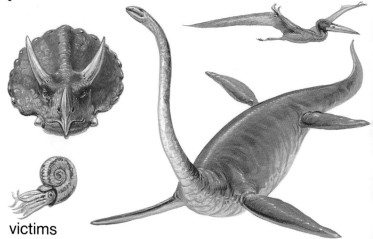

victims

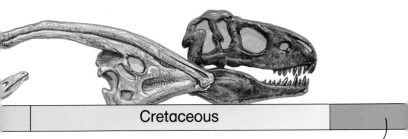

| | Cretaceous | |

CENOZOIC

But many other animals survived.
Insects, fish, frogs, birds and mammals are
still around today. So are some of the
reptiles: turtles, crocodiles, snakes and
lizards.

Scientists are trying to discover why the
dinosaurs became extinct.

survivors

What happened?

The death of the dinosaurs has always been a mystery. Ever since dinosaur bones were first discovered, people all over the world have tried to solve the mystery.

Some of the ideas or theories seem funny.
Some theories seem more likely.
But no one knows for certain which theory is right.

Perhaps dinosaurs were too stupid to survive. But if that were true, why did they live so long?

Perhaps mammals ate too many of their egg
But why didn't this happen earlier?

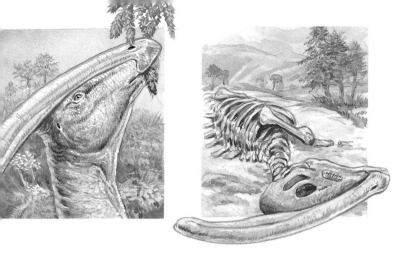

Many scientists wonder if the climate became cooler all over the Earth. Perhaps dinosaurs could not live without warmth.

Perhaps new plants poisoned the dinosaurs. But there were other plants to eat.

Perhaps they were too big. But the smaller ones disappeared too.

 # A big bang

Perhaps the dinosaurs were killed by an enormous asteroid. An asteroid is a rock that hurtles through Space. It is called a meteorite if it hits a planet.

Sixty-five million years ago a meteorite ten kilometres wide hit the Earth. This is what might have happened next...

The crash threw up a huge cloud of dust, high into the sky. The dust blocked out the sun. With no sunlight, the air became cold and plants died. The dinosaurs perished.

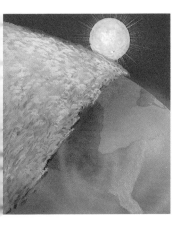

Mammals rule

The first mammals lived side by side with dinosaurs. But they did not become extinct at the end of the Mesozoic Era. Instead, they survived all through the Cenozoic Era, right up to today.

Plesiadapis lived in trees, like a monkey. It fed on insects.

Barylambda was larger and lived on the ground. It was a plant-eater.

After the dinosaurs disappeared, the mammals took over rapidly. Mammals are all warm-blooded and have fur or hair. We are mammals.

The first mammals were the size of rats. Soon larger mammals appeared: monkeys, pigs, horses, wolves and others.

The first big meat-eater was Andrewsarchus.

Hyracotherium was the first horse, but it was tiny. It fed on leaves in the forests.

Grazers and hunters

About 30 million years ago, a change took place. The first grasses appeared. Before then, plant-eaters had fed on leaves from trees. Now great prairies or grasslands spread around the world. New grass-eating mammals evolved.

Brontotherium

Archaeotherium

Poebrotherium

Palaeolagus

But as well as new plant-eaters, there were new and dangerous meat-eaters. Hoplophoneus was a cat that hunted small grazers. Cynodictis was a hunter too, but it was a dog. Gomphotherium was probably too big for either of them to attack.

Gomphotherium

Hoplophoneus

Cynodictis

Ice-age monsters

Several times during the last million years, much of Europe and North America became covered with ice. Mammals grew thicker coats of fur to keep warm.

woolly mammoths

Smilodon

The first humans evolved five million years ago. Now they hunted animals for meat.

woolly bison

There was no ice where these big animals lived.

giant kangaroo, Australia

moa, New Zealand

Amazing facts

The death of the dinosaurs at the end of the Mesozoic Era was not the biggest extinction of all time. Earlier, at the end of the Palaeozoic Era, two or three times as many species became extinct.

There are more than 100 theories for the extinction of the dinosaurs – so far!

Some scientists think that meteorites hit the Earth every 26 million years. If so, the next one is due in 13 million years' time.

One of the oldest groups of mammals is the primates. This group includes monkeys, apes and humans.

The largest mammal ever found was a long-necked rhinoceros called Indricotherium. It was over five metres tall and weighed about 30 tonnes. But that is still much smaller than the biggest dinosaurs.

Finding

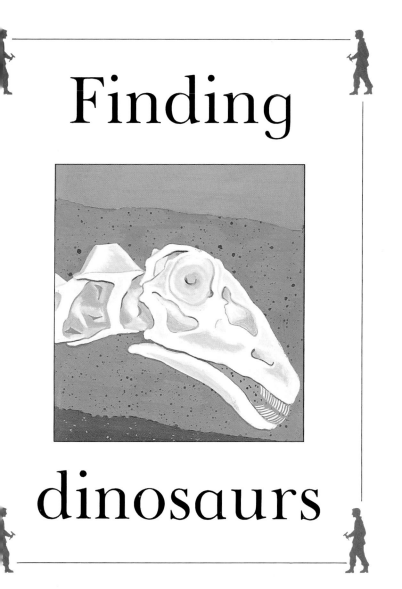

dinosaurs

The fossil hunters

People have known about dinosaurs for less than 200 years. Huge bones were dug up in quarries, but no one knew what they were. Were they the bones of elephants, or dragons, or giants?

Georges Cuvier

"reptiles"

In 1822 Georges Cuvier suggested that the bones might belong to giant reptiles.

William Buckland

Gideon & Mary Mantell

William Buckland was the first person to name a dinosaur. In 1824 he named Megalosaurus, meaning 'big lizard'.

Gideon and Mary Mantell were keen fossil hunters. In 1825, Gideon named a second dinosaur, Iguanodon.

In 1842, Richard Owen invented the word dinosaurs, or 'terrible lizards'.

More dinosaurs were discovered in North America – Othniel Marsh and Edward Cope found dozens from 1870 to 1900.

Richard Owen   Edward Cope   Othniel Marsh

"dinosaurs"

What is a fossil?

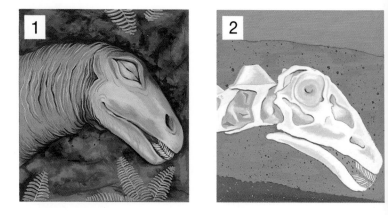

Dinosaur bones, footprints and other clues are all examples of fossils. Fossils are the remains of plants and animals from long ago. They are usually found in rock. How did they get there? Like this...

One hundred million years ago, Diplodocus died. After a few weeks its flesh rotted away, or was eaten. Later its bones were covered by sand or mud. This slowly turned to rock. Hard rock protects the bones. They have become fossils. Much, much later, a lucky find is made!

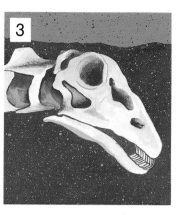

Some kinds of fossils show
us more than bones.
This spider got trapped
in sticky resin on a tree.
The resin turned into hard amber.

This mammoth was
frozen solid
thousands of years
ago in icy Russia.
It still has flesh
and hair.

Digging up dinosaurs

Palaeontologists look for dinosaurs in rocks of the right age. First, bulldozers take away a great deal of rock. Then small drills and brushes carefully remove rock around the bones. Maps are drawn to show where all the bones lie.

Next, workers cover the bones with strips of cloth dipped in plaster. The plaster makes a hard case to protect the bones. Then the bone parcels are loaded up. They are taken to a museum or a university for study in a laboratory.

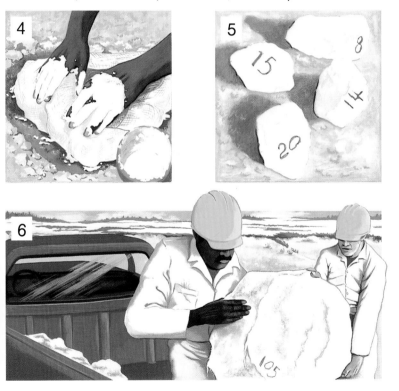

Building dinosaurs

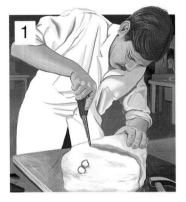

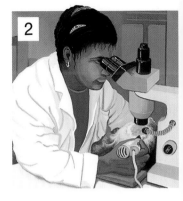

In the laboratory, technicians remove the plaster case with saws. Then they clean the bones carefully, often with a small drill, under a microscope. Next they coat the bones with varnish, to protect them from dust and dirt.

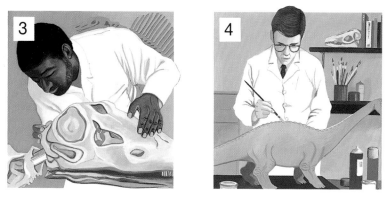

A dinosaur has over 300 bones! They are put together as a skeleton fixed on a metal or plastic frame. An artist makes a model to show what the dinosaur looked like.

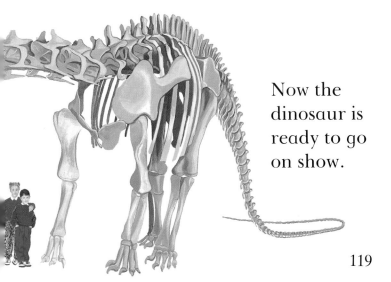

Now the dinosaur is ready to go on show.

Museums to visit

You can see dinosaur fossils and models at these museums:

Birmingham Museum and Art Gallery
Chamberlain Square, Birmingham B3 3DH

The Dinosaur Museum
Icen Way, Dorchester, Dorset DT1 1EW

Hunterian Museum
The University, Glasgow G12 8QQ

The Leicestershire Museums
96 New Walk, Leicester LE1 6TD

Museum of Isle of Wight Geology
Sandown Library, High Street, Sandown,
Isle of Wight PO36 8AF

The Natural History Museum
Cromwell Road, London SW7 5BD

The Royal Museum of Scotland
Chambers Street, Edinburgh EH1 1JF

Sedgwick Museum
Cambridge University, Downing Street,
Cambridge CB2 3EQ

University Museum
Parks Road, Oxford OX1 3PW

INDEX